BOOK ANALYSIS

Written by Verity Roat

The Woman in White

BY WILKIE COLLINS

WILKIE COLLINS

ENGLISH NOVELIST, PLAYWRIGHT AND SHORT STORY WRITER

- **Born in London (England) in 1824.**
- **Died in London (England) in 1889.**
- **Notable works:**
  - *No Name* (1862), novel
  - *Armadale* (1866), novel
  - *The Moonstone* (1868), novel

Wilkie Collins was the son of famous Royal Academician landscape painter, William Collins (1788-1847). He spent his early life living in London with his deeply religious family. Between 1836 and 1838 his family lived in Italy and France, which allowed him to become fluent in both Italian and French. On returning to England, he attended the Reverend Cole's private boarding school, where he was bullied by a boy who would force Collins to tell him stories before going to sleep. In later life, Collins attributed his discovery of his talent for story-telling to this time. After school, Collins decided to study law and was eventually called to the bar (although he never formally practised). In March 1951, Collins was introduced to Charles Dickens (English writer and social critic, 1812-1870), which helped him to further his writing career. Collins did not believe in the institution of marriage and instead split his time between Caroline Graves and Martha Rudd, his common law wife with whom he had three children. He died in 1889 following a paralytic stroke.

THE WOMAN IN WHITE

AN EARLY DETECTIVE NOVEL EXPLORING IDENTITY AND DECEPTION

- **Genre:** novel
- **Reference edition:** Collins, W. (2012) *The Woman in White.* [Kindle edition].
- **1st edition:** 1859-1860
- **Themes:** identity, morality and justice, power, gender, deceit and suspicion, family and marriage, mental illness, memory

The Woman in White was first published as a serial between 26 November 1859 and 25 August 1860. Whilst it contains many of the features associated with gothic novels, it is widely believed to be the first of the genre of 'sensation novels' and can be considered a precursor to detective fiction. The story centres on a tale of mistaken identity between Laura Fairlie, a wealthy gentlewoman, and the titular 'Woman in White' Anne Catherick, a poor, mentally ill woman. This turns out to be part of a plot devised by Laura's husband, Sir Percival Glyde, and his associate, Count Fosco, in order to obtain Laura's inheritance. The novel enjoyed commercial success during its own time, though some contemporary critics disliked it, and it continues to be regarded as Collins's best novel; Collins himself appears to have believed this too, as it is the only one of his novels which is mentioned in the epitaph on his gravestone.

SUMMARY

WALTER HARTRIGHT'S ARRIVAL AT LIMMERIDGE HOUSE

Walter Hartright, a young drawing master, is given a position at Limmeridge House in Cumberland, where he is to teach two young ladies to draw and to attend to the master of the house's archives. On his way to Cumberland, he meets a distressed young woman dressed entirely in white and helps her on her journey. He later overhears a policeman say that this woman has escaped from an asylum.

On arriving at Limmeridge House, he is introduced to his two pupils: the beautiful Laura Fairlie, the niece of his employer, Mr Fairlie, and Marian Halcombe, her devoted yet unattractive half-sister. Walter is astonished to discover the resemblance between Laura and 'The Woman in White', who is revealed to be Anne Catherick, a mentally disabled young woman who used to go to the school run by Laura's mother, to whom she was devoted.

LAURA'S MARRIAGE TO SIR PERCIVAL GLYDE

Over the coming months, Walter and Laura fall in love. Unfortunately, as Marian reveals to Walter, Laura is engaged to be married to Sir Percival Glyde, a baronet, who was a close friend of her father. Marian insists that Walter leaves Limmeridge to spare Laura any further embarrassment and upset. However, Laura receives an anonymous letter warning her not to marry Sir Percival. Walter deduces that the letter has come from Anne and concludes that it was Sir Percival who locked Anne up in the asylum. Laura consults with her family lawyer, who has concerns about the financial terms of the marriage settlement, as it allows Sir Percival to inherit all of Laura's fortune should she die first. Laura then confesses to Sir Percival that she is in love with another man. Despites these events, the two are married in December 1849 and honeymoon for six months in Italy. Walter, devastated by the loss of Laura, joins an expedition to Central America.

After their honeymoon, Laura and Sir Percival return to his house, Blackwater Park, with his friends Count Fosco and Countess Fosco, Laura's aunt. At Laura's request, Marian is sent for to join the two couples and she quickly overhears that Sir Percival is in debt. Sir Percival initially tries to bully Laura into signing a document which would allow him immediate access her inheritance of £20,000. After she refuses, Laura is contacted by Anne, who communicates that she knows a secret which would ruin Sir Percival's life. Their communication is discovered by Sir Percival before Anne can reveal the secret.

SWITCHED IDENTITIES

These events lead Sir Percival to become very paranoid and more desperate about his money woes, so Count Fosco suggests that they use the resemblance between Anne and Laura to their advantage. They plan to trick both women into travelling with them to London. Once there, they will place Laura in the asylum under Anne's name and Anne, who by this point is terminally ill, will be buried under Laura's identity when she dies. Marian overhears the plot, but contracts typhus after staying in the rain too long eavesdropping.

While Marian lays in bed too ill to move, Sir Percival and Count Fosco execute their deception exactly as planned. When she recovers, Marian visits the asylum and bribes the nurse into letting Laura escape. At the same time, Walter has returned from his expedition and the three live together in disguise. Marian and Walter work in order to make ends meet while Laura recovers from her trauma. During this time, Walter attempts to discover the truth about Sir Percival and Count Fosco's pasts so that he can blackmail them into confessing their crime.

SOLVING THE CRIME

In the course of Walter's research, he speaks to Anne's mother, who reveals that Anne did not know Sir Percival's secret as he believed. Walter travels to Old Welmingham, where Sir Percival was born, to further his research. Once there, he discovers Sir Percival's secret: his parents were not married when he was born, thus making him and his claim to his title, lands and fortune illegitimate. In order to conceal this fact, Sir Percival forged his parents' marriage on the register in the parish church. Meanwhile, Sir Percival finds out that Walter has discovered the secret. In order to destroy the evidence of his forgery, Sir Percival locks himself in the church and sets fire to the entries. The entire church catches fire and Sir Percival is killed. From the information he has gathered, Walter also surmises that Anne is the illegitimate daughter of Laura's father, thus accounting for their similarity.

Walter returns to London, determined to force a confession from Count Fosco. Walter hopes his old friend Pesca, a political refugee from Italy, will be able to identify the Count. Pesca does not recognise the Count, but Count Fosco is terrified when he sees him. After questioning Pesca about his past, Walter infers that Count Fosco was a member of the same secret society as Pesca. Walter confronts the Count and forces him to provide the evidence to prove Laura's identity. The Count goes into hiding in Paris, where he is eventually assassinated by a member of the secret society, and Laura and Walter, having now married, live happily with Marian. On the death of Mr Fairlie, they discover their infant son, also named Walter, has become the heir of Limmeridge House.

CHARACTER STUDY

WALTER HARTRIGHT

Walter Hartright, a young drawing master, is the narrator who begins the story of *The Woman in White.* The novel opens with Walter in strained financial circumstances, even though he is from a middle-class background and has recently secured a position as a drawing teacher at Limmeridge House through the recommendation of his Italian friend, Professor Pesca. Walter is brave, hard-working and diligent, and is the driving force behind the investigation of the mystery of the 'Woman in White'. He also takes on the responsibility of building a case to restore Laura's identity after her husband's fraudulent scheme to acquire her money. During this time, Walter assumes the somewhat patronising role of Laura's protector and infantilises her; for example, when Laura expresses a wish to contribute to their financial maintenance, he proposes that she draw pictures to sell. In fact, he collects these drawings from her and pays her from the wages he has earned, all the while pretending that he has sold them on to another buyer. In this way, he embodies the archetypal middle-class Victorian man; he takes on a paternal role with his wife, assumes all financial responsibilities and attempts to control his wife's feelings where he can.

FREDERICK FAIRLIE

Mr Fairlie is Laura's uncle and the guardian of her and Marian. He is incredibly wealthy, childless, unmarried and something of a hypochondriac; he is sensitive to all lights, sounds and smells and spends the majority of his time shut away in his bedroom. As such, he is incredibly selfish and self-absorbed and somewhat neglects his duties to Laura as a guardian and protector. Whilst Laura's marriage to Sir Percival Glyde was arranged by her father, Mr Fairlie is also in favour of it. When Laura becomes reluctant after receiving the anonymous letter, Mr Fairlie refuses to arrange a favourable marriage settlement for her and insists that the marriage should continue as planned. Furthermore, he is completely absorbed by his collections, including paintings, drawings and coins, which furthers his separation from the rest of society. Overall, Collins appears to be satirising the stereotype of the Victorian upper-class gentleman who is obsessed with aesthetics and fails to engage with the world around him. Ultimately, Mr Fairlie dies alone and Limmeridge House, his property, is inherited by Laura, through her son.

LAURA FAIRLIE

Laura is Mr Fairlie's innocent niece who is the heroine of the tale. She is an orphan and heiress to her uncle's property and money. At the beginning of the novel, she lives with her invalid uncle, Frederick Fairlie, and her elder half-sister, Marian. She is the embodiment of the Victorian ideal of femininity; she adores flowers and wearing white, and is beautiful and graceful. However, this makes her quite weak and forces her to rely on more masculine characters for help and protection, such as Marian, Walter and her lawyer. Early on in the narrative, she falls in love with her drawing master, Walter, but is betrothed to marry Sir Percival Glyde. Once married, Laura is completely dominated by her husband and his co-conspirator Fosco and her previous happiness and spirit are destroyed. She is incapable of protecting herself against her husband's plot and is imprisoned in an asylum under the guise of Anne Catherick as part of this plot. Throughout the novel, she encounters many trials which she is unable to overcome alone, making her the perfect damsel in distress.

MARIAN HALCOMBE

Marian is Laura's older half-sister from their mother's first marriage. When Walter first encounters her, he compliments her figure but is disappointed by her mannish demeanour and ugly face. She is a lot physically and mentally stronger than her younger sister; she makes frequent comments about her lack of femininity and how this enables her to be more strong-willed, intelligent and resourceful. She is fiercely devoted to Laura and even moves in with Laura after her marriage in order to protect her. Through the character of Marian, Collins is challenging the Victorian expectations of gender; she is often described as stronger than her male counterparts and plays a vital role in the narrative, as she helps Walter to discover the truth behind Anne Catherick's story and to build the case to restore Laura's identity. Her bravery and strength even attract admiration from Count Fosco, despite his seeming preference for weaker women like his wife. Marian is briefly separated from Laura because of her illness in the middle of novel, but by the end of the novel she and Laura have been reunited and it is said that Laura and Walter rely on her for the education of their son.

ANNE CATHERICK

Anne Catherick is the titular 'Woman in White' whom Walter encounters at the beginning of the novel. She bears an uncanny resemblance to Laura, due to their unknowingly being half-sisters. Sir Percival Glyde and Count Fosco take advantage of this later in novel when they switch the identities of the two women in order to gain access to Laura's inheritance. Anne's story is very tragic; she is the unwanted child of Jane Catherick and Laura's father, she is persecuted by Sir Percival when he believes she knows his secret and is therefore locked away in an asylum, and she ultimately dies of a fatal heart illness she has had for all of her life. Through Anne's mistreatment in the asylum, Collins explores the theme of mental illness.

MRS CATHERICK

Anne's mother. She helped Sir Percival Glyde to fake his claim to his inheritance and thus is controlled by him to ensure that she keeps his secret. She knew Laura's father and bore him an illegitimate child, Anne. She embodies the image of the scheming social climber of the Victorian era and delights in the expensive gifts which rich men, like Sir Percival, showered her with, as well as enjoying the respect of the society in which she lives.

SIR PERCIVAL GLYDE

Sir Percival is Laura's husband, despite being 20 years her senior, and one of the two important antagonists of the novel. He is the illegitimate child of a baronet and a low born woman and as such fakes his parents' marriage record to secure his possession of the baronetcy and property belonging to his late father. He is incredibly two-faced and scheming; when he first meets

Laura and Marian, he puts on the manners and charms expected of a wealthy, upper-class suitor. However, once married, he abandons all pretence and his treatment of Laura is representative of the abuse many women faced at the time. After his collusion with the Count to inherit Laura's money, he becomes increasingly paranoid and rushes to destroy his parents' marriage certificate with fire. In his haste, he locks himself in the church and the flames consume him. His death frees Laura and enables her to marry Walter.

COUNT FOSCO

Count Fosco is the second of the two important antagonists of the novel. He is an Italian exile who fled from Italy after betraying 'The Brotherhood' and is therefore wary of meeting any Italians in England. He is married to Laura's aunt and, like Sir Percival, is in a certain amount of debt which he hopes to alleviate through his wife's inheritance. He is in his sixties and obese, yet most women, Marian included, find that he has an oddly attractive quality. He is calculating and is therefore the mastermind behind the plot to switch Laura and Anne's identities. After he is discovered, he flees to Paris, where at the end of the novel it is stated that he is killed by a member of 'The Brotherhood'.

PROFESSOR PESCA

Pesca is Walter's friend and secures him the position at Limmeridge House. He features most prominently towards the end of the novel, when he reveals that he was exiled from Italy by the 'The Brotherhood', of which he is a member. This information proves to be essential to the plot as it helps Walter to discover Count Fosco's past.

ANALYSIS

GENRE: AN EARLY DETECTIVE NOVEL

The Woman in White is often heralded by modern critics as one of the first and finest examples of the Victorian sensation novel and, as such, can be considered a precursor of the modern detective novel. The book's genre is obvious from very early on in the novel, when Walter encounters the eponymous 'Woman in White' for the very first time:

> "[...] stood the figure of a solitary Woman, dressed from head to foot in white garments, her face bent in grave inquiry on mine, her hand pointing to the dark cloud over London, as I faced her." (p. 13)

From that moment, the reader's interest is piqued and the mystery of the novel is laid out: who is the 'Woman in White', why is she out alone in the dark and what role will she play in the novel? The mystery deepens further throughout the course of the events of the rest of the novel. Through Laura's marriage, her banishment to an asylum, her switching places with Anne Catherick and the Count and Sir Percival's mysterious pasts, the reader's attention is further captured.

The Woman in White can be considered a 'novel of incident'. In the mid-Victorian era, critics believed that novels must be based on either plot or character, and evidently it is the events of this novel that drive forward its plot. Nonetheless, Collins was believed to be able to also paint well-rounded characters, which gave his works their popularity. This genre became increasingly popular at this time due to its 'escapist' nature, as novels of this genre contain a "provision of an element of sensational mystery to readers whose real lives are anything but mysterious" (Hennelley, Jr, 1980: 452). The novel's plot balances the heart and the head through the presence of two detective forces: Walter's love for Laura and her lawyer's skill at his profession. Collins's own experience of the legal profession doubtlessly played a role in his expert writing of this novel. Whilst it is ultimately the Law which solves Laura's predicament by restoring her identity and eventually her fortune, Walter is the main detective of the novel. By using an average everyman character, Collins allows his readers to involve themselves in the narrative and play detective alongside Walter. The mystery of the 'Woman in White', Count Fosco and Sir Percival is slowly unravelled throughout the three epochs of the novel. This slow reveal of information is characteristic of this genre and permits the reader to form their own conclusions about the mystery, thus keeping them interested in the plot.

Finally, the very structure of the novel is indicative of the genre of detective fiction. The novel is presented as a collection of statements, very much like those given in a court case. This is reiterated by Walter's preface to the text, which states "No circumstance of importance, from the beginning to the end of the disclosure, shall be related on hearsay evidence." (p. 3). In setting the novel up in this way, Collins gives the illusion that this is a real case and thus increases the reader's interest in the events of the novel.

GENRE: ELEMENTS OF GOTHIC FICTION

Whilst this novel is undoubtedly a 'sensation' novel, there are some features which are characteristic of the Gothic genre which was prevalent at the time. The first appearance of the 'Woman in White' is incredibly gothic, as her white clothes give her the appearance of a ghost, characteristic of Gothic fiction.

Furthermore, Collins often makes use of pathetic fallacy (when the weather or atmosphere reflects the characters' mood or events of the plot), another feature of Gothic fiction. A good example of this is the scene in which Marian is eavesdropping on the Count and Sir Percival's conversation about their plot to switch Laura and Anne's identities:

> "'The rain has come at last,' I heard him say. It had come. The state of my cloak showed that it had been falling thickly for some little time."
> (pp. 230-231)

The presence of heavy rain and dark skies creates a sense of foreboding about the Count and Sir Percival's conversation and foreshadows the wrongdoings which they are conducting. As illness is also a common theme in Gothic fiction, Marian's typhus which develops after this event is also indicative of the genre.

Thus, although the main genre of the novel is 'sensation', Collins employs gothic elements to drive forward the plot and create atmosphere around dark moments of the novel.

GENDER

As Collins was an advocate for women's rights, it is perhaps unsurprising that the theme of gender features heavily in the novel. This is explored in two main ways: through Laura's marriages to Sir Percival and Walter and through Marian.

As previously stated, Laura is the embodiment of the weak damsel in distress who needs a man to save her, and given Collins' feminist leanings, it is perhaps surprising to find this archetype in one of his novels. Nonetheless, her relationships with the men in her life play a vital role in the exploration of gender, as she is a vehicle through which Collins highlights the unfair treatment of women in this era. At the beginning of the novel, she is subject to her hypochondriac uncle's will, because he is her guardian, and is thus forced to marry Sir Percival. After initially charming Laura during their courtship, his behaviour quickly turns after their marriage and he begins to mistreat her. He controls her and forces her to travel and live where he pleases. He then goes on to attempt to force her to sign over her fortune to him. When she is reticent and asks to read the document first, he replies "Nonsense! What have women to do with business? I tell you again, you can't understand it" (p. 171), thus highlighting the typical Victorian view that women are less intelligent than men. Thus far, Collins appears to be painting a typical picture of Victorian gender roles. However, his critique of this behaviour becomes evident through Laura's change in character. She becomes withdrawn and depressed and only comes out of this stupor when she is freed of Sir Percival and marries Walter, who treats her much more kindly. Whilst she is saved by a man, it highlights what may have been Collins's beliefs about how men should treat their wives.

Moreover, through Marian, Collins unpicks many of the stereotypes of Victorian women. Whilst Marian constantly berates herself for being "nothing but a woman" (p. 138), there are many favourable comparisons made by Marian and other characters between her character and appearance and that of a man's. For example, Count Fosco states that she has "the foresight and the resolution of a man" (p. 230) and this ultimately plays a vital role in the resolution of the mystery at the end of the novel. Without Marian's stoicism and intelligence, more typical of male characters of the mid-Victorian era, Walter would be unable to resolve the mystery and save Laura. As such, Collins highlights both that women can and in fact *should* be as strong as men. At the end of the novel, Marian lives happily as a single woman, having devoted her life to her sister. In this way, Collins may have been suggesting that a woman's life could have a different, equally valuable purpose other than fulfilling the stereotypical duties of wife and mother.

MENTAL HEALTH

Mental health is a key theme in *The Woman in White,* as both Anne and Laura are imprisoned in an asylum at different points in the novel. At the beginning of the novel, when Walter meets Anne Catherick for the first time, she is clearly very afraid of returning to the asylum, thus hinting at the poor treatment she has received there. Likewise, when Marian visits Laura in the asylum, she sees that she has become a shell of her former self, indicating the barbarity of the place.

Furthermore, when both women are believed to be mad, many of the other characters refuse to believe the truth about them. As a child, Anne's mother felt that she was mentally disabled and as such loathed and reviled her, particularly when she became obsessed with wearing white. She treated her poorly, half the time palming her off to a friend, Mrs Clements, and half the time insisting on being near her, but tormenting her by refusing to let her wear white and teasing her for her beliefs. When Anne parrots her mother's words about Sir Percival's secret, he believes she knows the whole secret, rather than just of its existence, and has her locked away, despite her mother's protestations. The letter which she sends to Laura to warn her about Sir Percival is dismissed by Sir Percival as the ramblings of a mad woman. Similarly, when Laura tries to prove to her gaolers that she is not Anne Catherick, they ignore her on the basis that she is 'mad'. As both Laura and Anne's sanity is proved by the end of the novel, Collins appears to be criticising the treatment of the mentally ill at this time.

FURTHER REFLECTION

SOME QUESTIONS TO THINK ABOUT...

- What affect does the presence of multiple narrators have on the believability of the novel? Is every narrator reliable?
- Compare *The Woman in White* to a modern detective novel of your choice. How can we see through this comparison that *The Woman in White* is a precursor to the detective genre?
- Is Laura's portrayal as a damsel in distress in conflict with Collins's own views on women? How would the novel be different if there was a stronger character, like Marian, as its protagonist?
- Explore the theme of sisterly love in the novel. How does it help to further the plot?
- Based on the following quotation, what is the reader's first impression of Anne Catherick?

> "She held a small bag in her hand: and her dress—bonnet, shawl, and gown all of white—was, so far as I could guess, certainly not composed of

very delicate or very expensive materials. Her figure was slight, and rather above the average height—her gait and actions free from the slightest approach to extravagance." (p. 14)

- How faithful is the BBC's 2018 adaptation of *The Woman in White* to the novel? Answer with reference to the genres of Gothic fiction and 'sensation' novels.
- Is the Law presented favourably in this novel? What do you think was Collins's opinion of contemporary lawyers?
- Does the portrayal of illegitimacy in *The Woman in White* fulfil your expectations of contemporary society's opinion of it?
- In what ways does Collins critique Victorian societal expectations of gender in this novel?
- How is the Foreign depicted in this novel? Compare and contrast the characters of Count Fosco and Pesca in your answer.
- How is the theme of class and wealth explored in *The Woman in White*?

We want to hear from you!
Leave a comment on your online library
and share your favourite books on social media!

FURTHER READING

REFERENCE EDITION

- Collins, W. (2012) *The Woman in White.* [Kindle edition].

REFERENCE STUDIES

- Hennelley, Jr, M. M. (1980) Reading Detection in *The Woman in White. Texas Studies in Literature and Language.* 22(4), pp. 449-467.

- Kendrick, W. M. (1977) The Sensationalism of *The Woman in White. Nineteenth-Century Fiction.* 32(1), pp. 18-35.

ADAPTATIONS

- *The Woman in White.* (1871) [Theatre]. Wilkie Collins.

- *The Woman in White.* (1912) [Film]. George Nichols. Dir. America: Gem Motion Picture Company.

- *The Woman in White.* (1929) [Film]. Herbert Wilcox. Dir. United Kingdom: British & Dominions Film Production.

- *The Woman in White.* (1948) [Film]. Peter Godfrey. Dir. America: Warner Bros.

- *The Woman in White.* (1997) [Television]. Tim Fywell. Dir. United Kingdom: BBC.

- *The Woman in White.* (2004) [Musical Theatre]. Trevor Nunn. Dir. United Kingdom: The Palace Theatre.

- *The Woman in White.* (2018) [Television]. Carl Tibbetts. Dir. United Kingdom: BBC.

MORE FROM BRIGHTSUMMARIES.COM

- Reading guide – *The Moonstone* by Wilkie Collins.

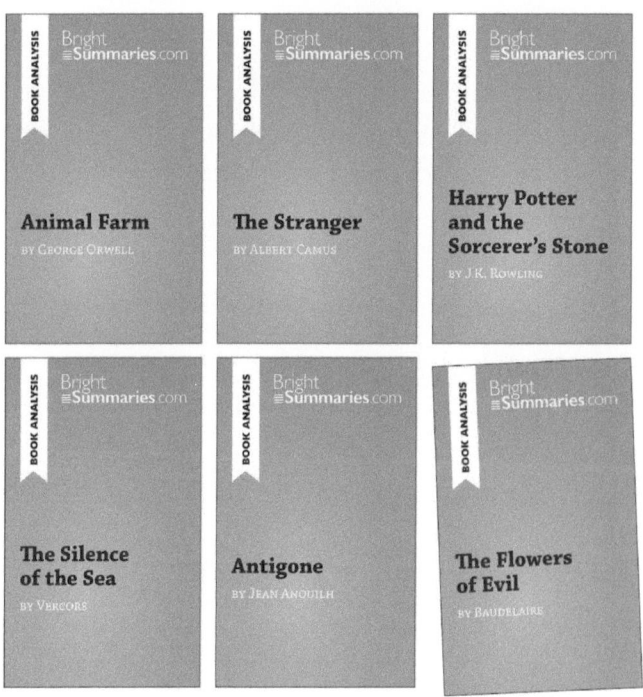

Although the editor makes every effort to
verify the accuracy of the information published,
BrightSummaries.com accepts no responsibility for
the content of this book.

www.brightsummaries.com

Ebook EAN: 9782808016278

Paperback EAN: 9782808016285

Legal Deposit: D/2018/12603/574

Cover: © Primento

Digital conception by Primento, the digital partner of
publishers.